Land, power and politics: the life and career of Odda of Deerhurst

by Ann Williams

Few English thegns can be so firmly associated with a particular place as Odda of Deerhurst; and few such places have preserved into the modern world so much of the physical fabric of his time. It is an especial pleasure to me to be able to speak on his family and career in the church which he would have known, and where he came to worship, and close to the site of the manor-house in which he lived, and the chapel which he built in his brother's memory; and I should like to begin by thanking Michael Hare and the Friends of Deerhurst Church for giving me this unique opportunity.[1]

The known facts of Odda's life are few, though relatively abundant in comparison with most of his peers. Since he enters the historical sources in 1013 as an adult, he was presumably born in the closing decades of the tenth century, surely no later than 993.[2] From 1013 to 1050 he appears regularly among the thegns who attest the royal charters of successive kings, and he also witnesses charters and memoranda for the bishops of Sherborne, Winchester and Worcester.[3] In 1051, when Earl Godwine of Wessex and his family were exiled by the Confessor, Odda was made earl of the western shires (Dorset, Somerset, Devon and Cornwall), previously incorporated into Godwine's earldom.[4] In 1052, King Edward had a royal fleet assembled at Sandwich, and gave joint command to his nephew Ralph, earl of the east midlands and of Herefordshire, and to Earl Odda.[5] William of Malmesbury adds that both Odda and Ralph were kinsmen (*cognati*) of the king.[6] Their remit was to prevent Godwine, who had taken refuge in Bruges, from staging a come-back. What followed is best related in the contemporary account of the 'E' version of the *Anglo-Saxon Chronicle*, which was being compiled at St Augustine's, Canterbury:

Then Earl Godwine went out from Bruges with his ships to the Isere, and put out to sea a day before the eve of the midsummer festival [23 June], so that he came to Dungeness, which is south of Romney. Then it came to the knowledge of the earls out at Sandwich, and they then went out in pursuit of the other ships, and a land force was called out against the ships. Then meanwhile Earl Godwine was warned; and he went to Pevensey, and the storm became so violent that the earls could not find out what had happened to Earl Godwine. And then Earl Godwine put out again so that he got back to Bruges, and the other ships went back again to Sandwich. Then it was decided that the ships should go back to London, and that other earls and other oarsmen should be appointed to them. But there was so long a delay that the naval expedition was quite abandoned and all the men went home.[7]

The dispersal of the royal fleet encouraged Godwine to try again, and this time he was successful; his display of power, and the support he received in the south-east forced the king to reinstate him. The south-western shires reverted to the West Saxon earldom, but Odda did not lose his rank; he was compensated with an earldom in the west midlands, encompassing Worcestershire and perhaps Gloucestershire as well.[8] He continued to be active in this region until 1056, when he died, on 31 August, at his manor of Deerhurst, having been professed a monk by Ealdred, bishop of Worcester. He was buried at Pershore Abbey. Both Pershore and the priory of Great Malvern, Worcs, remembered Odda as a benefactor, and he built the church of Holy Trinity, Deerhurst, in memory of his brother Ælfric.[9] The 'D' version of the *Anglo-Saxon Chronicle* describes him as 'a good man and pure and very noble', an appreciation elaborated by the twelfth-century historian John of Worcester: 'the lover of churches, succourer of the poor, defender of widows and orphans, helper of the oppressed, guardian of virgins'.[10] The inscription in his lead coffin, discovered at Pershore in 1259, calls him *cultor Dei*, 'a labourer for God'.[11]

So much (or so little) has already been established, but three areas repay further research: Odda's family, his landed wealth and his place in the local society of western and south-western England in the eleventh century.

1. *Odda's family.*
Odda's brother Ælfric is remembered in the dedication of Holy Trinity, Deerhurst, founded in his memory. His death at Deerhurst, on 22 December 1053, and his burial at Pershore are recorded both in the 'D' version of the *Anglo-Saxon Chronicle* and by John of Worcester.[12] Domesday Book reveals the existence of Odda's sister, Eadgyth, who held land at Upleadon, Herefds.[13] Whether she outlived her brothers is uncertain, for not all Domesday's pre-

Conquest landowners were holding on 5 January 1066 ('the day when King Edward was alive and dead'). When Odda died without heirs, his estates were appropriated by King Edward, and Upleadon too may have passed through the king's hands, for in 1086 it belonged to Albert the Lotharingian, one of the Confessor's chaplains who later served the Conqueror. If Eadgyth held Upleadon as her brother's tenant (which would not be unusual), her land too would have gone to the king when Odda died.[14]

Odda's siblings are recorded but not his parentage and here we pass into the realms of uncertainty. The starting-point must be William of Malmesbury's description of Odda as a kinsman (*cognatus*) of Edward the Confessor. A second clue is to be found in the late-medieval annuals of Pershore, now represented only by extracts made in the sixteenth century by the antiquary John Leland.[15] The Pershore annals record Odda as a benefactor who restored to the abbey the lands seized by his predecessor, the wicked earl *Delfer*. Elsewhere Leland preserves a short set of laconic annals, possibly from the same source, which name Odda as *Elfer*'s son.[16]

Earl *Delfer* or *Elfer* must be Ælfhere, ealdorman of Mercia, whose reputation as a despoiler of churches sprang from his political rivalry with St Oswald, bishop of Worcester.[17] Since Ælfhere died in 983, he was probably not the father of Odda, who first appears in 1013. Indeed their kinship may be a simple assumption on the part of the Pershore annalist, based on nothing more than the fact that both exercised authority in the west midlands. Historians, however, have been reluctant to abandon their alleged relationship, for Ælfhere is addressed as a kinsman by contemporary West Saxon kings, and a descendant of his would therefore be related to King Edward.[18] The relationship would be rather remote but Edward had few male kinsmen of any kind and thus every reason to make the most of what remained to him.[19]

Some years ago, I suggested that Odda was more likely to be related to Æthelweard, ealdorman of the Western Shires from 973 to c.998. He is known as Æthelweard the Chronicler, from his Latin translation of a version of the *Anglo-Saxon Chronicle*, and in the course of this work, he tells us that he was a descendant (a great-great-grandson) of King Æthelred I.[20] This hypothesis has not as yet found favour, but I should like to propose it again, in greater detail. There are, I think, several indications of this relationship, some of which are only significant in the context of the whole, and the accompanying family-tree [Table 1] may help to illuminate the sometimes tortuous lines of argument.

The most technical piece of evidence may be disposed of first. Odda first appears in the historical record as a witness to three charters dating from the end of Æthelred II's reign, one for each of the years 1013, 1014 and 1015.[21] The witness-lists of royal charters represent the more important of those who, from time to time, attended the king's court. At first sight, they present merely a bewildering jumble of unfamiliar names, but the determined eye can discern significant patterns. It has been shown that members of the same family tend to be grouped together; and that newcomers to the various ranks of the king's entourage (bishops, abbots, ealdormen and thegns) usually attest at the bottom of the appropriate list, gradually moving up as they acquire seniority.[22]

Seen in this light, Odda's first attestations are very interesting. In the first place he is given some prominence among the thegnly witnesses, the *ministri*.[23] In 1013 he is third among eleven *ministri*; in 1014, he is fifth among nine; and in 1015 he is the second of four. Such prominence suggests the influence of a powerful kindred. In the 1014 charter, the third thegnly witness, two places above Odda, is Godwine. He has a common name (two other Godwines attest Æthelred's charters), but this particular Godwine can be identified as one who attests regularly from 996 to 1016. He is probably the Godwine killed in the latter year at the battle of *Assandune*, and was almost certainly one of Ealdorman Ælfhere's nephews.[24]

This might seem to confirm the Pershore tradition that Odda was a kinsman of Ælfhere. However both in 1013 and in 1014, Odda is immediately preceded by one Ælfgar, who can be identified as the west country thegn, Ælfgar *mæw* ('Seagull').[25] Ælfgar *mæw*'s memory was preserved in the traditions of the religious houses founded or patronized by his family, at Tewkesbury, Gloucs, and Cranborne, Dorset. Ælfgar and his mother Ælfgifu, widow of Æthelweard *mæw*, are named in a charter of Æthelred II, dating from 1000 and confirming the gifts they have made to

Cranborne Abbey; and the Tewkesbury chronicle, written around 1200, adds that Ælfgar's father, Æthelweard *mæw*, was related to the West Saxon royal house.[26] Æthelweard was a very common name at the turn of the tenth and eleventh centuries, but the only royal kinsman known to have borne it was Æthelweard the Chronicler, who died c.998. Odda's appearance in the witness-lists next to Ælfgar *mæw* suggests their kinship, and if Ælfgar's father really was Æthelweard the Chronicler, then they were kin to Æthelred II as well.[27]

This may seem too much to deduce from a pair of attestations to two charters but there are other indications of relationship. The first concerns Æthelweard's ealdordom. On Æthelweard's death c.998, his office as ealdorman of the western shires passed to his son Æthelmær. Æthelmær died in or soon after 1013, and the western shires passed to his son-in-law, another Æthelweard, who was exiled by Cnut in 1020.[28] Cnut then gave the western shires to his own brother-in-law, Godwine, who was already earl in the south-east, thus creating the earldom of all Wessex, held in turn by Godwine and by his son Harold, King Harold II. It is therefore of interest that, when Godwine fell from power in 1051, the king should have given the western shires to Odda; was he reviving the interests of a family which had once wielded authority in that region, but which had lost out to the powerful lord whom the king wished to be rid of?

The second clue relates to Pershore Abbey. The original community seems to date back to the seventh century, but its subsequent history is obscure until its re-establishment as a Benedictine abbey in the late tenth century. King Edgar's charter of re-endowment, dated 972, is an eleventh-century forgery, but William of Malmesbury records the Pershore tradition that its patron at this time was Ealdorman Æthelweard.[29] As we have already seen, Odda too was remembered at Pershore as a benefactor, and both he and his brother Ælfric were buried there. Thus Odda can be associated with a man who is possibly Æthelweard's son, with the ealdordom which Æthelweard held, and with one of the abbeys which he patronized.

I would maintain that these connections are at least suggestive of a blood relationship between Æthelweard the Chronicler, the great-great-grandson of King Alfred's brother Æthelred I, and Odda of Deerhurst, *cognatus* of Edward the Confessor, the son of King Alfred's great-great-grandson, Æthelred II. What that relationship might be is difficult to say. It seems unlikely that Odda was a son of Ealdorman Æthelmær, for if so surely he, rather than Æthelmær's son-in-law, would have received his earldom after his death. Æthelweard himself, however, had a brother, Ælfweard, and a sister Ælfwaru, either of whom might be a parent or grandparent of Odda.[30]

The search for Odda's parentage demonstrates the major problem in tracing early medieval families. Only from the later middle ages was it customary for individuals to bear two names, a personal Christian name, and an inherited surname, indicating the family to which they belonged. In early medieval Europe, surnames were not used; each individual had only one name (an idionym), and kinship was signalled in other ways than a common family name.[31] Some kindreds used recurring idionyms; thus the pre-Conquest dukes of Normandy were called William, Richard or Robert, whereas their neighbours, the counts of Anjou, favoured Fulk or Geoffrey. In much the same way, English families used a set of recurring name-elements. The West Saxon royal dynasty favoured the first elements *æthel* - ('noble') and *ead* - ('prosperity, wealth'): hence Æthelred, 'noble counsel', Eadweard, 'prosperous guardian' and so forth. Ealdorman Æthelweard was, to judge from his *Chronicle*, inordinately proud of his royal kinship, and signalled this pride in the name he chose for his son, Æthelmær, incorporating (as does his own) the favourite royal element *æthel* -, also found in the name of his mother Æthelgifu. The name of Odda's sister Eadgyth incorporates another favoured element, and that of his brother Ælfric shares its first element with another royal name, Alfred (Ælfræd). No English king was called Odda, but John of Worcester says that Odda had another name; he was also called Æthelwine.[32]

Odda is not the only possesser of two names in eleventh-century England, but it is rarely possible even to guess why the second name was chosen.[33] Since Odda was (if only briefly) earl of the western shires, it may be significant that an earlier official in the region was also called Odda; it was he who, as ealdorman of Devon, captured the Raven banner from a force of Vikings in 878.

His exploit is recorded both in the *Anglo-Saxon Chronicle* and in Asser's *Life of Alfred*, but his name is recorded only in the version of the *Anglo-Saxon Chronicle* translated into Latin by Ealdorman Æthelweard.[34] It seems at least possible that the earlier Odda was among their ancestors, and that this is why Odda of Deerhurst took his second name.[35]

2. Odda's estates.

Though Odda's wealth is better-documented than his ancestry, its full extent cannot be estimated, for, since he died in 1056, his lands are recorded only sporadically in our main source for the estates of King Edward's thegns, Domesday Book. We may assume that Deerhurst itself was one of his manors; it was assessed at 119 hides of land, 60 hides of which belonged to the church of St Mary, Deerhurst.[36] Odda also held Longdon, Worcs, assessed at 30 hides, and Mathon, assessed at 5 hides, one of which lay in Herefordshire.[37] We should probably include his sister Eadgyth's manor of Upleadon, Herefords, assessed at 9 hides, in his estate, and he may also have held Poltimore, Devon, assessed at just under 4 hides in 1086.[38] This gives Odda a minimum of 167 hides of land in four shires. It is misleading to use the Domesday valuations for the pre-Conquest period, but for what it is worth they yield a figure of £143.1s.[39] Possession of such an estate (which represents only the minimum of Odda's wealth) would place him twenty-ninth out of the 90 thegns identified as holding lands worth £40 or more on the eve of the Conquest.[40] Such men are described in contemporary sources as *proceres* ('chief men') or *optimates* ('the best men'); we may as well call them magnates.

The description of Odda's manors in Domesday allows us to see something of their structure and organization. Mathon, the smallest, belonged to Pershore Abbey by 1066 (see Table 2). Four of its five hides lay in Worcestershire and a fifth lay in Herefordshire. It is the Herefordshire folios which reveal Odda's tenure of the manor, for this hide had been divided by 1086 between two holders, Roger de Lacy, in succession to Merewine, and Drew fitzPons, in succession to Alweard. Both Merewine and Alweard are described as thegns (*teini*) of Earl Odda, and of each it is said that 'he could not withdraw without his lord's permission'.[41] This limitation shows that the lands were thegnland, belonging to the lord of Mathon, and granted to his men in return for service.[42] The word 'thegn' means 'servant' (Latin *minister*) and the English aristocracy as a whole was a service-aristocracy, in which status was defined not only by birth and wealth, but by the status of the lord to whom service was due: thus the laws of Cnut distinguish between the king's thegn, who served the king, and the median thegn, who served some other lord. Merewine and Alweard fall into the second category.[43]

Mathon was a small, compact manor, but Deerhurst and Longdon were very different in structure and size. Deerhurst is described by Domesday in exceptional detail. Like many large estates, its lands did not constitute a discrete bloc of territory. There was a central core, close to the vill of Deerhurst itself, but attached to this were a number of outlying vills, scattered over north Gloucestershire and into the neighbouring shires of Worcester and Warwick. It seems that on Odda's death without heirs, his lands passed to his kinsman the king, who eventually divided the estate at Deerhurst between his own abbey at Westminster, and his physician Baldwin, a monk of Saint-Denis, Paris, to which Baldwin's share of Deerhurst eventually passed (see Table 3).[44] Each share included part of the central core of land, plus a number of outlying vills; Kemerton was actually divided (unequally) between the two. C.S. Taylor showed, many years ago, that this division corresponded to the earlier division between the secular estate held by Odda himself (which went to Westminster) and the land belonging to the minster church of St Mary (which went to Baldwin, and thence to Saint-Denis).[45]

The structure of Odda's estate at Deerhurst is shown in Table 4. The chief vill, the 'head-manor' (*heafodbotl, caput manerii*), which gave its name to the whole estate, is Deerhurst itself, where Odda's manor-house or *burh* would have stood, presumably close to Odda's chapel, the estate-church as opposed to the ancient minster.[46] To this were appurtenant four dependent vills or berewicks, only one of which (Hardwicke) lay within the central core of land; the others were outlying vills. With the head-manor, these berewicks constituted the demesne, the lands actually owned by the lord.[47] To the demesne were attached lands held by others but owing rents and services to the lord of the head-manor; I will return to these in a moment. The 60 hides of Deerhurst which belonged to Saint-Denis in succession to St Mary's, Deerhurst, are not described in such detail, but the same general structure can be seen (Table 5). The 'head-manor' here, of course, is the church of St Mary itself.

Longdon, which by 1086 had passed to Westminster Abbey, is smaller than Deerhurst, but resembles it in organization (Table 6). Its description in Domesday is less explicit, in that the names of the tenanted lands are not supplied but must be deduced from other sources; those that can be identified lay in Staunton, Eldersfield, Birtsmorton, Chaceley and Pull Court.[48] As at Mathon, Odda's tenure of Longdon is not noticed in the main entry for the manor, but in the Herefordshire folios, which reveal that Pull Court had 'lain in Earl Odda's manor of Longdon' before William fitzOsbern, earl of Herefordshire from 1067 to 1071, had attached it to Bushley; Earl William also removed the revenues of Eldersfield from Longdon and attached them to his castle at Hereford.[49]

Let us look more closely at Domesday's description of Odda's manor of Deerhurst (Table 4). For the sake of convenience I have labelled all the lands held by named tenants as 'tributary lands'. It is not unusual to find that some of these lands lay in the same vills as the demesne berewicks (see Bourton and Toddenham) and it is possible that in these cases (and perhaps others) we are dealing with *lænland*, land belonging to the lord but granted to his men for a limited term, usually life or a succession of lives, in return for service; but Domesday gives no details of the specific tenures. Other lands were attached to the head-manor in the sense that they owed what Domesday calls *consuetudines* ('customary dues') or *servicia* ('services'), but were owned by their holders. Such land could be sold or bequeathed or otherwise disposed of, provided that the *consuetudines* continued to be paid to the lord of the manor, as landlord (*landhlaford* or *landrica*).[50] The holders might be the commended men of their *landrica*, in which case he was also their *hlaford* or personal lord, but they were free to commend themselves (that is, to choose another personal lord) elsewhere if they wished.[51] This had actually happened at Deerhurst. In 1086, the largest tenement in Kemerton (Kemerton 3 on Table 4) was held, with Boddington, by Gerard the chamberlain. The entry for Deerhurst says of these lands that they 'always paid geld and did other services (*servitia*) in Deerhurst hundred, but after Gerard had them, they rendered neither geld nor service'.[52] To discover what had happened we have to turn to the description of Tewkesbury, which reveals that the pre-Conquest holder of Kemerton and Boddington, called Ljotr, had commended himself to Beorhtric son of Ælfgar, lord of Tewkesbury, and his land and service had been appropriated (illegally) by Beorhtric's post-Conquest successors.[53]

The holders of Deerhurst's tributary lands are described as 'radcnihts, that is free men', who 'ploughed, harrowed, scythed and reaped' for their landlord's benefit. Similar services were due from the free men (*liberi homines*) at Longdon, who owed one day's haymaking 'and did such other services as were required of them'.[54] Radcnihts, or radmen as they are also called, were mounted retainers, the successors of the men described as *geneatas* in pre-Conquest sources.[55] Though the radcnihts were non-noble free men and fell into the category of ceorls, not thegns, their obligations resemble those of the lesser thegns, and the line between them was not hard and fast. Thus the two radmen who, in the Worcestershire account, held the Herefordshire portion of Mathon are described as Earl Odda's *teini* in the Herefordshire folios. Alweard of Mathon is probably identical with the Alweard who held land at Longdon and who, as Alweard of Longdon, witnessed a charter of the bishop of Worcester in company with his lord, Earl Odda, Odda's brother Ælfric and 'all the leading thegns in Worcestershire'; the date must be 1051-2.[56] It is probable that most, if not all of the men who held lands at Deerhurst and Longdon in 1066 had originally been associated with Odda, but only in the cases of Alweard and Merewine do we have direct evidence.

3. Odda and his locality.

Odda's wealth would have made him a great lord in the western shires, a dispenser of patronage to laymen and ecclesiastics alike. Naturally it is his beneficence to the church that is best recorded. The monks of Pershore, as we have seen, remembered him as a second founder, restorer of the abbey's fortunes after its alleged spoliation at the hands of Ealdorman Ælfhere. It is unfortunate that the abbey's history after the refoundation of c.970 is obscure. There was a disastrous fire, perhaps in 1002, which may have led to a temporary cessation of religious life.[57] It seems that at least part of the endowment of Pershore came into Odda's hands at that time. His manor of Longdon is included among the lands allegedly granted to Pershore by King Edgar, and though the charter recording the grant is an eleventh-century forgery, Longdon probably did form part of the tenth-century endowment.[58] The annals of Pershore give 1020 as the date for the abbey's restoration after the fire, which is close to the moment of Odda's own emergence onto the public stage.[59] The abbey was functioning in the 1020s, when its abbot was Brihtheah, nephew of Wulfstan Lupus, archbishop of York and bishop of Worcester; Brihtheah himself was bishop of Worcester from 1033 to 1038. Presumably Odda restored Longdon to Pershore either in 1020, or on his death in 1056. Mathon, however, which does not appear in the foundation charter, was probably given to Pershore by Odda himself.[60]

The monks of Pershore believed that Odda had taken a vow of chastity, so that no heir should survive to despoil the church of its inheritance. Alas! Odda's death without heirs brought his property into the possession of his kinsman the king. Towards the end of his life, the king bestowed two-thirds of Pershore's Worcestershire lands upon his own abbey at Westminster, though the gift probably took effect only in the reign of William I.[61] The late J.H. Round attempted to absolve King Edward from the charge of despoiling Pershore to enrich Westminster, but the Confessor did not in the eleventh century have the saintly reputation which he later enjoyed, largely through the efforts of the Westminster monks themselves.[62]

The other Worcestershire house associated with Odda is the priory of Great Malvern, close to his manor of Longdon. The beginnings of the priory are lost in obscurity, but later tradition assigned the gift of its site, with 'the wood there as far as *Baldeyate*', to Earl Odda.[63] *Baldeyate* is presumably the lost 'Baldenhall' in Great Malvern parish, given to the hermits of Malvern by Edward the Confessor and confirmed by William I and subsequently by Henry I.[64] Aldwine, who originally founded Great Malvern as a hermitage, is said to have experienced many problems (not least, perhaps, the loss of his patron) and after many years of labour, decided to abandon the project and make the pilgrimage to Jerusalem. He was dissuaded by Wulfstan, bishop of Worcester from 1062 to 1095, from whom he had received the monastic habit; Wulfstan prophesied the future success of the community, and persuaded Aldwine to persevere.[65] Malvern does not appear in

Domesday Book, though woodland in Malvern Chase was appurtenant to the manor of Ripple, belonging to the bishop of Worcester, but it was flourishing by the 1090s, when it was home to the Lotharingian astronomer, Walcher (d.1125).[66] By this time, it was a dependency of Westminster Abbey.

Odda's relations with the church of Deerhurst are perhaps most interesting of all, but are not easy to reconstruct. St Mary's was an old minster church, dating back at least to the early ninth century.[67] Ælfheah (St Alphege), the archbishop of Canterbury murdered by the Danes in 1012, spent some part of his early career there but apart from this its early history is unknown.[68] How and when the church and its estate came into Odda's hands is unknown; it would be nice to think that he was the host when Edmund Ironside and Cnut held their peace conference at Alney by Deerhurst after the battle of *Assandune* in 1016.[69]

Odda's patronage of Deerhurst can be paralleled by that of his putative kinsmen at the minster of Tewkesbury. The Tewkesbury Chronicle says that the church was re-established by Æthelweard *mæw*, and it was further endowed by Æthelweard's son, Ælfgar; after Ælfgar's death (which must have occurred before 1040 at the latest) church and land passed to his son Beorhtric. Unlike that of Odda, Beorhtric's estate was intact on the eve of the Conquest and Domesday gives a detailed description of his great manor at Tewkesbury.[70] As at Deerhurst, the manor was divided between Beorhtric's secular estate and the land of the church, but the provision for the latter was much less generous, only 20 hides out of the total assessment of 95 hides, whereas St Mary's retained 60 of the manor of Deerhurst's 119 hides.[71]

Many of the minsters founded in the eighth century had subsequently experienced hard times. Some had fallen victim to the Viking raids of the ninth century, their communities dispersed or diminished and their lands appropriated by the West Saxon kings, either for their own enrichment and that of their followers, or for the endowment of the Benedictine abbeys founded or re-founded in the tenth century.[72] The examples of St Mary's, Deerhurst and the church of Tewkesbury suggest that some minsters were appropriated by up-and-coming lay magnates; they may indeed have been the foundation of such peoples' fortunes.[73]

The church of Holy Trinity at Deerhurst, which Odda built in memory of his brother Ælfric, was neither a minster, nor an abbey, nor a hermitage, but was intended to serve the lord's hall and the estate dependent upon it.[74] Such estate-churches were proliferating in the tenth century, so much so that Edgar legislated on their relationship with the minsters into whose parishes they intruded. The main disputes were over tithe and burial-fees: if the estate-church had a graveyard, the lord could divert one-third of his demesne-tithes to its support; if not, the whole tithe went to the minster and the lord could 'pay what he chooses to his priest from the [remaining] nine parts'.[75] The eleventh century saw no diminution in the building of such churches; indeed it probably intensified, reaching a climax in the decades on either side of 1100. Such churches, each served by a single priest, formed the basis for the later parochial organization.[76] Odda's church at Deerhurst, dedicated by Bishop Ealdred of Worcester on 12 April 1056, is almost exactly contemporary with the church at Kirkdale, rebuilt from its ruins by the Yorkshire magnate Orm Gamel's son 'to Christ and St Gregory, in the days of King Edward and in the days of Earl Tostig', that is, between 1055 and 1065.[77]

Odda clearly had a close relationship with the bishops of Worcester. Brihtheah, Pershore's first known abbot after the eleventh-century restoration, had been a monk of Worcester, and indeed became bishop in 1033. Between 1038 and the early 1050s, Odda attests charters of Brihtheah's successors, bishops Lyfing and Ealdred, all of which were grants of *lænland* to local thegns.[78] He also attests a grant of *lænland* in Oxfordshire made by Ælfwine, bishop of Winchester, in 1043 or 1044.[79] He may have been the donor to Worcester of 'Odda's book', recorded in an undated list of volumes belonging to the cathedral library. Unfortunately no indication of its contents is given but the other volumes in the list are all devotional in nature: a passional, the Alfredian translation of Gregory the Great's *Dialogues* (two copies), a martyrology, two psalters, Alfred's translation of Gregory's *Pastoral Care* (two copies), St Æthelwold's translation of the Benedictine Rule and the *vision* of St Barontus (d.700).[80] All were apparently in English, and given Odda's reputation for piety, he is quite likely to have had a personal copy of some devotional work in English for his private use.[81]

Perhaps the most interesting transaction involving Odda is the agreement between Bishop Ælfwold of Sherborne and Kari son of Toki, made before the shire-court of Devon in 1046.[82] This agreement, concerning land at Holcombe Rogus, Devon, was witnessed by the most important members of the shire–court, including its president, Earl Godwine; the first lay witnesses (in order of their appearance) are Odda, his brother Ælfric, Ordgar, Ordgar's brothers, Ælfgar and Osbearn, and Dodda *cild*. Odda, Ordgar, Ælfgar and Dodda reappear, along with Beorhtric son of Ælfgar, among a group of noblemen attesting charters of King Edward between 1042 and 1050.[83] Like Odda and (perhaps) Beorhtric, Ordgar was related to the king. He was probably the grandson of Ordgar of Devon, founder of Tavistock Abbey, whose daughter Ælfthryth married King Edgar, and became King Edward's grandmother. The family had land in Devon, still in the hands of Ordgar's son Ordwulf on the eve of the Norman Conquest.[84] Dodda *cild* is less well-attested, but his byname indicates a man of rank, and (like Odda) he was associated with the bishops of Worcester. He received land at Cutsdean, Worcs, from Bishop Brihtheah, and at Bredon's Norton from Ealdred, and also held of the church of Worcester at Sedgeberrow; the tenancies at Cutsdean and Sedgeberrow were inherited by his son Beorhtric.[85]

The existence of such groups of noblemen, related both to each other and to the king, throws some light on the functioning of royal power and of local society in the eleventh century. One of the sadder aspects of the Norman Conquest is that in sweeping away so completely the upper ranks of the Old English aristocracy, it has come to conceal such local societies from us, both as general groups, and as particular individuals and families. Rarely in works of general history do we meet with the great nobles of pre-Conquest England; indeed before the eleventh century, even the ealdormen are often little more than names. Yet there is no reason to suppose that they were any less significant in the reigns of Æthelred II or Edward the Confessor than in those of John, or Henry III, or the Yorkist and Lancastrian kings.

There was also until quite recently a feeling that since the pre-Conquest aristocracy came to grief in 1066, there was little purpose in studying it; that, having no future, it could have no past. Fortunately there were always historians, many of them local historians, who swam against the tide, and in recent years, it has shown distinct signs of turning; soon, perhaps the pre-Conquest nobles will be restored to their rightful place in the counsels of the king, and in the local business of the shires in which they lived. Only in the course of detailed investigation into such figures as Odda of Deerhurst can we come to understand something of the lost politics of the late Old English state.

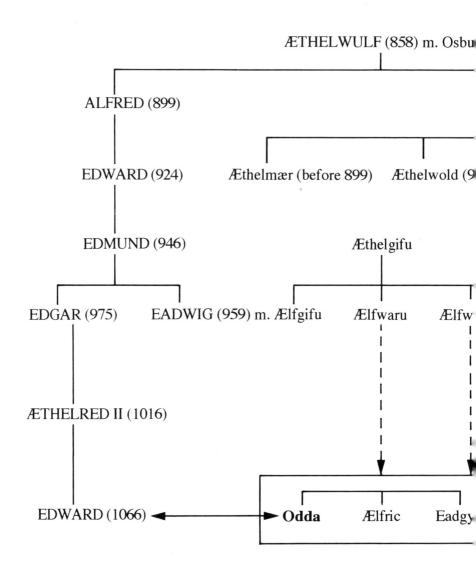

ÆTHELWULF (858) m. Osbu

ALFRED (899)

EDWARD (924)   Æthelmær (before 899)   Æthelwold (9

EDMUND (946)   Æthelgifu

EDGAR (975)   EADWIG (959) m. Ælfgifu   Ælfwaru   Ælfw

ÆTHELRED II (1016)

EDWARD (1066) ◄————————► **Odda**   Ælfric   Eadgy

TABLE 1. A hypothetical pedigree for Earl Odda.

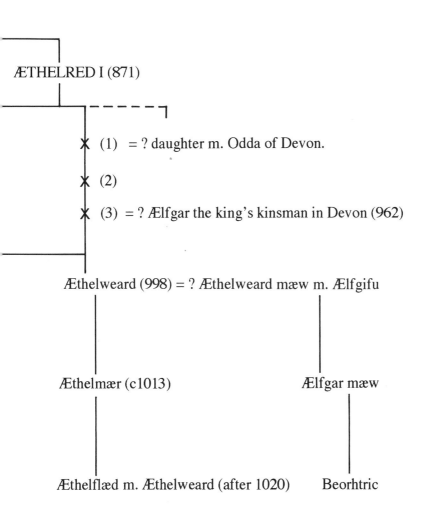

ÆTHELRED I (871)

(1) = ? daughter m. Odda of Devon.

(2)

(3) = ? Ælfgar the king's kinsman in Devon (962)

Æthelweard (998) = ? Æthelweard mæw m. Ælfgifu

Æthelmær (c1013)   Ælfgar mæw

Æthelflæd m. Æthelweard (after 1020)   Beorhtric

KEY
KINGS in capitals
Dates of death in brackets
Broken lines = hypothetical links

Table 2. The manor of Mathon	
Land	**Holders 1066**
3 hides	Pershore Abbey [Odda]
3 virgates	not named (Urse d'Abetot of Pershore, 1086)
1 virgate	not named (Walter Ponther of Pershore, 1086)
1 hide in Herefordshire	2 radmen, i.e. Merewine and Alweard, *teini* of Earl Odda
Total: 5 hides	

Table 3. Deerhurst divided	
1. Westminster (Odda)	2. Saint-Denis (St Mary's)
a) The 'central core'	
Deerhurst	
Hardwicke	Uckington
Elmstone	Staverton
Ellings	Haw
Wightfield	Leigh
Hayden	Walton
Evington	
Oridge	
Rye	
Hasfield	
b) the 'outliers'	
Upper Lemington	Coln St Dennis/Calcot
Todenham	Woolstone
Bourton-on-the-Hill	
Moreton-in-the-Marsh	
Sutton-under-Brailes (Warks)	Little Compton (Warks)
	Welford-on-Avon (Warks)
	Preston-on-Stour (Warks)
Kemerton (Worcs)	Kemerton (Worcs)

Table 4. The manor of Deerhurst: Odda			
Caput	**Berewicks**	**'Tributary lands'**	**Holders 1066**
Deerhurst			Westminster
	Hardwicke		Westminster
	Bourton 1		Westminster
	Todenham 1		Westminster
	Sutton (Warks)		Westminster
		Bourton 2	Wulfwig
		Todenham 2	Eadwig
		Elmstone	Beorhtric
		Ellings	Godric
		Wightfield	Eadwig
		Hayden	Wulfwig
		Evington	Alwig
		Oridge	Leofwine
		Rye	Eadric
		Hasfield	Beorhtric
		Lemington	Auti
		Moreton	Alfrith
		Kemerton (Worcs) 1	Leofwine
		Kemerton 2	Alwine
		Kemerton 3	[Ljotr]
		Boddington	[Ljotr]
Total: 5 hides	Total: 25 hides	Total: 29 hides	

Table 5. The manor of Deerhurst: St Mary's

Demesne	'Tributary lands'	Tenants
Uckington		
Staverton		
Coln St Dennis and Calcot		
Little Compton (Warks)		
Preston-on-Stour (Warks)		
Walford-on-Avon (Warks)		
Haw ('2$^1/_2$ hides beyond the Severn')		
[4$^1/_2$ hides of the above]		5 free men
	Leigh	1 free man
	Walton	
	Woolstone	
	Kemerton (Worcs)	
Total: 52$^1/_2$ hides	Total: 7$^1/_2$ hides	

Table 6. The manor of Longdon

Caput	'Tributary lands'	Tenants 1066
Longdon		Pershore Abbey [Odda]
	[Eldersfield]	Regenbald
	Pull Court	Ælfric
	[Staunton]	Alric
	[unidentified]	Godric
	[Birtsmorton]	Alwig
	[Chacely]	Alweard, Beorhtric, Alwig, Godric
	[Chambers Court]	as above
	[unidentified]	as above
Total: 11 hides	Total: 19$^1/_4$ hides	

Land, power and politics: the family and career of Odda of Deerhurst

Abbreviations.

Regesta   *Regesta Regum Anglo-Normannorum*, i, ed. H.W.C. Davis, ii, ed. C. Johnson and H.A. Cronne, iii, ed. H.A. Cronne and R.H.C. Davis (Oxford, 1913-68).

S.   P.H. Sawyer, *Anglo-Saxon Charters: an annotated list and bibliography* (London, Royal Historical Society, 1968).

FOOTNOTES

1.   I should also like to thank Michael Hare for all his help in preparing this lecture for publication, and especially for his numerous insights, comments and corrections, which have enabled me to improve and extend its coverage; all remaining errors of fact and judgement are, of course, my own responsibility.

2.   For Odda's earliest appearance, see below, pp. 4-5.

3.   For Odda's attestations to royal charters, see Simon Keynes, *An atlas of attestations in Anglo-Saxon Charters, c. 670-1066* (Cambridge, 1995), tables LXIII, LXIV, LXX, LXXV, LXXVIII; for the episcopal charters, see below, notes 78-9, 82.

4.   *The Anglo-Saxon Chronicle*, ed. and tr. D. Whitelock *et al.* (London 1961) [hereafter *ASC*], 'E', 1052.

5.   For Ralph, see David Bates, 'Lord Sudeley's ancestors: the counts of Amiens, Valois and the Vexin in the eleventh century', *The Sudeleys: lords of Toddington*, The Manorial Society of Great Britain (London, 1987), pp. 34-48; Ann Williams, 'The king's nephew: the family and career of Ralph, earl of Hereford', *Studies in medieval history presented to R. Allen Brown*, ed. Christopher Harper-Bill, Christopher Holdsworth and Janet L. Nelson (Woodbridge, 1989), pp. 327-43.

6.   William of Malmesbury, *De gestis regum Anglorum*, ed. William Stubbs, Rolls series (London, 1887) [hereafter *GR*], i, p. 243.

7.   *ASC* 'E', 1052.

8.   A. J. Robertson, *Anglo-Saxon Charters* (Cambridge, 1956), pp. 456-8.

9.   See below, p. 5.

10.   *ASC* 'D', 1056; *The Chronicle of John of Worcester*, ed. R.R. Darlington and P. McGurk (Oxford, 1995) [hereafter *JnW*] ii, pp. 580-1. As it stands the D Chronicle was written towards the end of the eleventh century, from earlier material which is probably more nearly contemporary with the events described (see Patrick Wormald, *How do we know so much about Anglo-Saxon Deerhurst?* ante, 1993, 13-17 and notes). John of Worcester was writing in the early part of the twelfth century, and based his early material on an *Anglo-Saxon Chronicle* related to D.

11.   *Odda dux quondam, priscis temporibus Ædwinus vocatus in baptismo, cultor Dei, monachus effectus ante mortem suam, hic requiescat. Sit et gaudium in pace cum Christo, Amen (Johannis Lelandi antiquarii de rebus Britannicis Collectanea,* ed. Thomas Hearne (London, 2nd ed., 1770), vol. Ii, p. 244). The coffin was discovered 'on the day after the feast of St Barbara' (i.e., either 5 or 16 December), during the laying of a new pavement in St Mary's Chapel. On the following day the coffin of the first post-reform abbot, Foldbriht, was found next to that of Odda, but both had been moved at least once, after the 'second fire', presumably the one in 1223. Leland's source was the Pershore annals (now lost), see below, note 15. John of Worcester gives Odda's 'baptismal' name as Æthelwine (see note 32 below).

12.   *ASC* 'D' 1053, *JnW* ii, pp. 574-5.

13.   *Great Domesday, a facsimile,* ed. R.W.H. Erskine (London, 1986) [hereafter *GDB*], fo. 186; *Domesday Book: Herefordshire,* ed. Frank and Caroline Thorn (Chichester, 1983) [hereafter *DB Herefords*], no. 18,1.

14.   The sister of the Devonshire magnate, Ordwulf (for whom see note 84 below) held of her brother at Croyde (*GDB*, fo. 105; *Domesday Book: Devonshire,* ed. Caroline and Frank Thorn (Chichester, 1985) [hereafter *DB Devon*], no. 15,41 and note).

15.   Leland, *Collectanea,* ed. Hearne, vol Ii, pp. 242-4; also printed by W. Dugdale, *Monasticon Anglicanum,* ed. J. Caley, H. Ellis and B. Bandinel (London, 1817-30) [hereafter *Monasticon*], ii, p. 415.

16.   *The itinerary of John Leland,* ed. L.T. Smith (Oxford, 1907-10), 3, p. 39 (in the edition of Thomas Hearne (Oxford 1769), the reference is vol. 2, Book V p. 2).

17.   Whether Ælfhere really despoiled Pershore of its lands is outside the scope of this lecture and, in view of the loss of virtually all the early documentation relating to the abbey, must remain not proven (A. Williams, '*Princeps Merciorum gentis*: the family, career and connections of Ælfhere, ealdorman of Mercia, 956-83', *Anglo-Saxon England* 10 (1982), pp. 143-72).

18.   Robertson suggests (*Anglo-Saxon Charters,* pp. 457-8) that Odda was Ælfhere's grandson; see also Robin Fleming, *Kings and lords in Conquest England* (Cambridge, 1991), p. 51.

19.   Æthelred II had six sons and at least three daughters by his first wife, and two sons and a daughter by Emma of Normandy, his second. Athelstan, the eldest son, died on 25 June 1014, and three of his brothers, Ecgberht, Eadred and Edgar, probably also predeceased their father (Simon Keynes, *The diplomas of Æthelred II 'the Unready', 978-1016* (Cambridge, 1980), p. 267 and Table 1). Edmund Ironside, who succeeded in 1016, died in the same year from wounds received at the battle of *Assandune* and his infant sons were smuggled from England to save them from death at the hands of Cnut, who had Edmund's surviving brother, Eadwig, exiled and (probably) murdered. Edward the Confessor's full brother Alfred was murdered in 1036 by Cnut's son and

successor, Harold I. The Confessor's full sister, Gode, had two children by her French husband, Drogo count of Amiens, one of whom (Earl Ralph) accompanied Edward to England in 1042. Of Edward's half-sisters, one became abbess of Wherwell and another married Eadric Streona, ealdorman of Mercia; her grandsons, Siward and Ealdred, are described as the king's kinsmen in Domesday Book and by the twelfth-century historian Orderic Vitalis (*GDB* fo. 179v; *The ecclesiastical history of Orderic Vitalis*, ed. Marjorie Chibnall, ii (Oxford, 1990), pp. 194-5). The third sister married Uhtred of Bamburgh, earl of Northumbria, but the stormy political relations between Bamburgh and the West Saxon kings did not encourage either party to remember their kinship; Uhtred's grandson, Gospatric, was in the entourage of Tostig, earl of Northumbria and son of Earl Godwine of Wessex (Ann Williams, *The English and the Norman Conquest* (Woodbridge, 1995), 29-30). Robert fitzWymarc and his son Swein are described as King Edward's kinsmen; since Robert seems also to have been related to Duke William, the connection was probably through Edward's mother, Emma of Normandy (*The life of King Edward the Confessor*, ed. Frank Barlow (London, 1962), p 76. F.E. Harmer, *Anglo-Saxon Writs* (Manchester, 1952), pp. 357-8, 571, 573). Wigod of Wallingford, an important landholder in the south midlands, is also addressed as a kinsman by Edward, but the nature of their relationship is unknown (Harmer, *Anglo-Saxon Writs*, pp. 368-70, 577).

20. Ann Williams, 'An introduction to the Gloucestershire Domesday', *The Gloucestershire Domesday*, ed. Ann Williams and R.W.H. Erskine (London, 1989), p. 28. For Æthelweard, see *The Chronicle of Æthelweard*, ed. A. Campbell (London, 1962) and Robertson, *Anglo-Saxon Charters*, pp. 386-7.

21. C.R. Hart, *The charters of Barking Abbey* (London, forthcoming), no. 11; S.933, 934.

22. Keynes, *The diplomas of Æthelred II*, pp. 154-62, 188-9, 209-13.

23. Keynes, *An atlas of attestations*, table LXIII (3), (6), (9).

24. *ASC*, 1016; this Godwine is described as ealdorman of Lindsey (see also Williams, 'Princeps Merciorum gentis', pp. 169-72).

25. Keynes, *The diplomas of Æthelred II*, pp. 209, 227 note 265.

26. C.R. Hart, *The early charters of eastern England* (Leicester, 1966), pp. 253, 254 (the charters are now lost and survive only in eighteenth-century transcripts); *Monasticon* ii, p. 54.

27. Williams, 'An introduction to the Gloucestershire Domesday', pp. 21-2; Ann Williams, 'A west-country magnate of the eleventh century: the family, estates and patronage of Beorhtric son of Ælfgar', *Family trees and the roots of politics*, ed. K.S.B. Keats-Rohan (Woodbridge, forthcoming).

28. Ealdorman Æthelmær is not heard of after he led the western thegns to submit to Swein Forkbeard in 1013 (*ASC*, 1013). He may have been the father of Æthelnoth, archbishop of Canterbury from 1020-38 (*JnW*, ii, pp. 506-7; M.K. Lawson, *Cnut: the*

Danes in England in the early eleventh century (London, 1993), pp. 148, 176). For his son-in-law, the younger Æthelweard, see Simon Keynes, 'Cnut's earls', *The reign of Cnut*, ed. Alexander Rumble (Leicester, 1994), pp. 67-70. Ealdorman Æthelmær has been identified with Æthelmær *se græta*, whose son (yet another Æthelweard) was murdered by Cnut (*ASC*, 1017), but despite the fact that the ealdorman is called *le Grete* and *Grossus* in the Cartulary of Eynsham Abbey (which he founded), I still believe (as did A.J. Robertson, see *Anglo-Saxon Charters*, pp. 130, 376, 387) that Æthelmær *se græta* was a different person, Æthelmær son of Æthelwold (who occurs c. 990 as Æthelwold *se greta*). This Æthelmær attests charters of Æthelred II from 999-1009 (Keynes, *The diplomas of Æthelred II*, pp. 204-10).

29.   S.786; William of Malmesbury, *De gestis pontificum Anglorum*, ed. N.E.S.A. Hamilton, Rolls series (London, 1870), p. 298. William calls Æthelweard 'earl of Dorset'.

30.   They are recorded in the will of their sister Ælfgifu, the former wife of King Eadwig (S.1484). Ælfgifu also mentions her sister-in-law Æthelflæd, but does not say to which of her brothers she was married.

31.   Cecily Clark, 'Onomastics', *The Cambridge history of the English language*, ed. Norman Blake (Cambridge, 1992), pp. 551-2.

32.   *JnW* ii, pp. 580-1. The Pershore annals give his baptismal name as Eadwine, incorporating the *ead-* element (see note 11 above).

33.   Mannig, abbot of Evesham (1044-58), was also called Wulfmær, and Ealdred, abbot of Abingdon (1066-71), was called Beorhtwine (*JnW* ii, pp. 540-1; *Chronicon monasterii de Abingdon*, ed. Joseph Stevenson, Rolls Series (London, 1858), i, p. 486).

34.   *ASC* 878; Simon Keynes and Michael Lapidge, *Alfred the Great* (Harmondsworth, 1983), pp. 84, 248; Æthelweard, *Chronicle*, p. 43. Æthelweard does not spell out the details of his descent from Æthelred I (Æthelweard, *Chronicle*, p. 39). Æthelred I is known to have had two sons, Æthelmær, who was probably dead by 899, and Æthelwold, killed in 903 disputing the kingship with his cousin, Edward the Elder. Æthelweard does not record this incident, which has suggested to some that he was a descendant of the rebellious ætheling. It might be, however, that Æthelweard was descended from a daughter of the king, married to Odda of Devon, a shire with which Æthelweard's family is closely associated. John of Worcester describes his son Æthelmær as earl of Devon (*JnW* ii, pp. 474-5), and he had property at Upottery, Devon, which he bartered for land on which to found his abbey at Eynsham, Oxon (S.911). One of the intervening generations might be represented by Ælfgar 'the king's kinsman in Devon', whose death in 962 is recorded in the *Anglo-Saxon Chronicle*; he and his brother Byrhtferth were prominent at the court of King Eadwig (955-59), whom Æthelweard, in contrast to the monastic writers, describes (*Chronicle*, p. 55) as one who 'deserved to be loved'. Ælfgar attests S.651 (958) as 'the king's kinsman' (Barbara Yorke, 'Æthelwold and the politics of the tenth century', *Bishop Æthelwold: his career and influence* (Woodbridge, 1988), p. 75 and note 90).

35.   In the discussion which followed the delivery of this paper, Michael Hare advanced another intriguing explanation for Odda's name. It is, of course, the English equivalent of the widespread continental name which appears variously as Odo in west Frankia, Otto in east Frankia ('Germany'), and Ottar in Scandinavia. Thus in the *Anglo-Saxon Chronicle* for 982, which records the Emperor Otto II's expedition to southern Italy, the emperor's name, along with those of his nephew, Duke Otto of Swabia and his father, Otto I, is rendered Odda. This entry, which represents Otto II's disastrous defeat by the Sicilian Moslems as a victory, may have been composed by Æthelweard himself, for his own *Chronicle* was dedicated to Matilda, abbess of Essen, the sister of Duke Otto of Swabia, who died in the course of the 982 campaign (L. Whitbread, 'Æthelweard and the *Anglo-Saxon Chronicle*', *EHR* 74 (1959), pp. 577-80). Æthelweard was writing his *Chronicle* in the 980s, around the probable time of Odda's birth, and given his connections with the German imperial family, a child born to him, or to one of his near kindred, might well be given a name which reflected the pretensions and interests of his family at that time. Odda's sister Eadgyth (Edith) too has the same name as the daughter of King Edward the Elder who married Otto I, and whose son Liudolf was father both to Duke Otto of Swabia and Matilda of Essen. For Æthelweard's contacts with Abbess Matilda, see Elisabeth van Houts, 'Women and the writing of history in the early middle ages: the case of Abbess Matilda of Essen and Æthelweard', *Early Medieval Europe* 1 (1992), pp. 53-68.

36.   *GDB*, fo. 166; *Domesday Book: Gloucestershire*, ed. John S. Moore (Chichester, 1982) [hereafter *DB Gloucs*], nos. 19,1-2; 20,1.

37.   *GDB*, ff. 174v, 175v, 184v, 186; *Domesday Book: Worcestershire*, ed. Frank and Caroline Thorne (Chichester, 1982) [hereafter *DB Worcs*], nos. 8,9; 9,6; *DB Herefords*, nos. 10,39; 23,6.

38.   For Upleadon, see note 14 above. Poltimore is described as *manerium Odonis* in Domesday Book; in 1066 the greater part of the manor (just under $3\frac{1}{2}$ hides) had belonged to Beorhtric (perhaps Beorhtric son of Ælfgar) and Scireweald and another half-hide was held by Wulfmær *cot* (*GDB*, ff. 107, 117v; *DB Devon*, nos. 16, 90:92; 50,l). For Odda's connection with Devon, see below, p. 14.

39.   The figures for pre- and post-Conquest values in Domesday (expressed as *valuit*, 'it was worth' and *valet*, 'it is worth') are probably an estimate of what the estate would fetch if it was 'farmed'; i.e., let out for a fixed annual sum to a tenant (or 'farmer'), who would recoup his outlay from the actual renders of the estate. The 'values' are different from the 'renders' (*reddebat, reddet* in Domesday), which represent actual sums received, rather than estimates; where both are recorded, the 'render' is usually larger than the 'value'. In the case of Odda's estate at Deerhurst (see Table 4) Domesday gives the pre-Conquest 'render', not the 'value': 'in the time of King Edward the whole manor gave as farm (*dabat de firma*) £41 and 8 sesters of honey by the king's measure'. In adding 'renders' to 'values' we are not adding like to like, but the 1086 *valet* of the manor was £40 (*GDB* fo. 166; *DB: Gloucs*, no. 19,2).

40.   Peter A. Clarke, *The English nobility under Edward the Confessor* (Oxford, 1994), pp. 32-3. Odda does not, of course, figure in Dr. Clarke's total, since his full holding cannot be determined.

41.   *GDB* ff. 184v, 186; *DB Herefords*, nos. 10,39: 23,6.

42.   Unlike *lænland*, also granted by the lord in return for service (see note 54 below), thegnland usually consisted of a small estate, and was probably held by members of the lord's immediate entourage as a consequence of their duties in that lord's service, as cook, huntsman, military retainer or the like.

43.   II Cnut, 71-71.5 (*English Historical Documents, volume 1: c.550-1042*, ed. Dorothy Whitelock (London, 1955) [hereafter *EHD* i], p. 429). See also the king's thegn who 'himself had a thegn who served him' (*Gethynctho* [The 'promotion' law], *EHD* i, p. 432). For Merewine and Alweard, see below, p. 10.

44.   A charter of William I, dated 1069 (*Regesta* i, no. 26) conveys to Saint-Denis the church of Deerhurst, as it was given by King Edward to Baldwin; Baldwin, by now abbot of Bury St Edmund's, still held land attached to St Mary's in 1086 (*GDB*, fo. 166; *DB Gloucs*, no. 19,2 and notes). Taynton, Oxon, also given to Saint-Denis by the Confessor, had also passed through Baldwin's hands (S.1028, 1105 and see Margaret Gelling, *The early charters of the Thames Valley* (Leicester, 1979), pp. 142-4). Baldwin, former prior of the cell of Saint-Denis at *Lebraha* (Leberaw) in Lotharingia, had apparently been sent to England precisely to look after the abbey's English interests, and continued to administer its properties here even after he was appointed abbot of Bury St Edmunds in 1065. Through him the cult of St Edmund became popular at Saint-Denis (Lindy Grant, 'Abbot Suger and the Anglo-Norman world', *Anglo-Norman Studies* 19 (1997), forthcoming; my thanks to Dr Grant for permission to cite her paper before publication).

45.   C.S. Taylor, 'Deerhurst, Pershore and Westminster', *Transactions of the Bristol and Gloucestershire Archaeological Society* 25 (1902), pp. 230-50.

46.   Domesday calls such places the *caput manerii*, 'head of the manor', translating OE *heafodbotl*, 'head-dwelling',

47.   See the pre-Conquest survey of Tidenham, Gloucs (Robertson, *Anglo-Saxon Charters*, pp. 204-7), whose structure would never be guessed from the laconic entry in Domesday (*GDB* fo. 164; *DB Gloucs*, no. 1,56), which does not even mention, let alone name the berewicks.

48.   *DB Worcs*, no. 8,9 and notes.

49.   *GDB* fo. 180v; *DB: Herefords*, nos. 1,44;46. Bushley lay in Worcestershire, but its revenues (like those of Eldersfield) had been attached to Earl William's castle at Hereford. The pre-Conquest tenant was Beorhtric son of Ælfgar, lord of Tewkesbury.

50.   Domesday sometimes describes such land as *libera terra*, 'free land', or says that it was held *libere*, 'freely'; in the northern and eastern shires, where the Domesday commissioners were more concerned than those elsewhere to record manorial structures, such land is called sokeland. The *landrica*'s rights over the tributary lands are expressed as 'sake and soke', and arose from the royal charter (or *landboc*) which recorded the king's grant of the estate, and of the royal rights (excepting military

service and the more important judicial dues) issuing from the lands appurtenant to it; estates held by such charters were called bookland. See the discussion in Williams, *The English and the Norman Conquest*, pp. 73-6 and the references there cited.

51. The *landrica* or *landhlaford* ('landlord') was entitled to the dues from the tributary estates, regardless of who held them, or to whom they were commended; the *hlaford* ('lord') held the personal commendation of his men, whether they held land of him or not (see the reference in the previous footnote).

52. *GDB* fo. 166; *DB: Gloucs*, no. 19,2.

53. *GDB* 163v, *DB Gloucs*, no. 1,41. After 1066, Tewkesbury passed in turn to William fitzOsbern, earl of Herefordshire (d. 1071), Queen Matilda (d. 1083) and the king. It was perhaps the queen who had given Kemerton and Boddington to Gerard. Such appropriations were not uncommon either before or after 1066, although commendation alone did not imply title to the land of the *commendatus*; title was conferred through succession to the *landrica* who had sake and soke, signalled by the render of *consuetudines*.

54. The services due from lands granted by the lord as *lænland* and land owing *consuetudines* (sokeland) are much the same; the difference between them lies in the land's status, *lænland* being the property of the lord and 'tributary' land (sokeland) of its holders. For the possible distinction between *lænland* and thegnland, see note 42 above.

55. In the pre-Conquest survey of Tidenham, Gloucs, each *geneat* 'must labour either on or off the estate, whichever he is bidden, and ride, and furnish carrying-service, and supply transport and drive herds and do many other things' (Robertson, *Anglo-Saxon Charters*, pp. 206-7). Similar duties were imposed on the lesser thegns; the median thegn, for instance, 'attended his lord in the king's hall and [went] on his errand to the king', whereas the king's thegn 'served the king and went in his household band on his errands' (*Gethynctho*, *EHD* i, p. 432). See also the services due from the thegns who held *lænland* of the church and bishopric of Worcester (*Hemingi Chartularium Ecclesie Wigornensis*, ed. Thomas Hearne (Oxford, 1723), pp. 292-6, translated in R. Allen Brown, *The origins of English feudalism* (London, 1963), pp. 132-4).

56. S.1409; Robertson, *Anglo-Saxon Charters*, pp. 208-9, 459. Ælfweard's name is too common for further identification, but Earl Odda's *teinus* Merewine is probably the Merewine who held land in Archenfield, Herefords, and perhaps in Warwickshire also; he was still holding his Warwickshire estate in 1086 (*GDB* ff. 184, 240, 244, *DB Herefordshire*, no. 1,54; *DB Warwickshire*, nos. 16,35; 37,7).

57. The undated annals (Leland, *Itinerary*, 3, p. 39) place the burning-down of the monastery and its abandonment by the monks after Odda's restoration of the lands seized by his 'father', Earl *Elfer*, but the sequence of events is more likely to have been reversed. The date of 1002 for the fire is given by *Monasticon* iii, 410, but on what basis is unclear (see also note 59 below).

58.   S.786, dated 972. For the purposes of local administration, the bulk of Pershore's Worcestershire land, including Longdon, formed a single unit of 300 hides, a triple hundred, like that of Oswaldslow, belonging to the bishopric of Worcester. Unlike the other Worcestershire hundreds, those of Pershore and Oswaldslow were not discrete blocks of territory, but consisted of the scattered holdings of the respective churches, which, since they interpenetrate one another, must have been formed at the same time, probably by King Edgar in the 970s (see Ann Williams, 'An introduction to the Worcestershire Domesday', *The Worcestershire Domesday*, ed. Ann Williams and R.W.H. Erskine (London, 1988), pp. 15-7). Longdon must thus have belonged to Pershore in King Edgar's reign.

59.   1020, *introitus fuit Persorensis novae ecclesiae post combustionem* (Leland, *Collectanea*, ed. Hearne, vol. Ii, p. 242; see also note 57 above).

60.   One of the very few early charters in the Pershore cartulary is S.932, dated 1014, Æthelred II's grant of 4 hides at Mathon to Leofwine, ealdorman of the *Hwicce* (printed in H.P.R. Finberg, *The early charters of the west midlands* (Leicester, 1961), pp. 145-6). The *Hwicce* included Worcestershire, Gloucestershire and part of Warwickshire, and since Odda was earl in the same area from 1052-56, the manor may have come to him in virtue of his office. On the eve of the Conquest it lay in the hundred of Doddingtree, the only one of Pershore's Worcestershire estates to lie outside the triple hundred of Pershore (see note 58 above).

61.   Harmer, *Anglo-Saxon Writs*, pp. 328-9, 330-2, 363-6. For the division   of Pershore's 300 hides between the abbeys of Westminster and Pershore, see *GDB*, ff. 174v-175 (*DB Worcs*, nos. 8,1-28); *GDB* ff. 175-175v (*DB Worcs*, no. 9,1-6). Pershore still had churchscot from the whole 300 hides, 'namely, from each and every hide where a free man dwells (*manet*) one packload of corn at Martinmas'.   The judicial dues were divided, one-third to Pershore, two-thirds to Westminster (*GDB* 175v; *DB Worcs*, no. 9,7).

62.   *Victoria History of the County of Worcestershire,* i, pp. 257-9. The Ramsey Chronicle records that Edward had to be bribed to confirm one of its estates (*Chronicon Abbatie de Rameseie*, ed. W. Dunn Macray (London, Rolls Series, 1886), p. 170).

63.   Odda's grant is recorded only in the thirteenth century, when he appears as *Hudde*, earl of Gloucester (*Monasticon*, iii, p. 448; *The register of Bishop Giffard*, ed. J.W. Willis Bund, Worcester Historical Society, 1902, p. 178; *VCH Worcs* ii, p. 137) .

64.   *VCH Worcs* iv, pp. 125-6. The only surviving charters are the confirmations of Henry I, dated 1127 (*Regesta* ii, nos. 1489-90; *Monasticon*, iii, pp. 447, 448). Edward's grant is there described as '*Baldeh* in the fee of Hanley', i.e. Hanley Castle, and that of William I as 'l virgate in *Baldehalla*'. In 1086, the revenues of Hanley Castle had been attached to the castle of Hereford, though it had once been tributary to Tewkesbury, Gloucs, held by Odda's putative kinsman, Beorhtric son of Ælfgar (*GDB*, ff. 163v, 180v; *DB Gloucs*, 1,34; *DB Herefords*, 1,42); among its appurtenances was 'a villan at *Baldehalle* rendering 2 ores of pence' (32d).

65.   The Worcester annals give the date of the priory's foundation as 1085, presumably after Wulfstan's exhortations (*The Vita Wulfstani of William of Malmesbury*, ed. R.R. Darlington, Camden Society third series 40 (1928), pp. xli-xlii, 26).

66.   R.W. Southern, *Medieval Humanism* (Oxford, 1970), pp. 166-8.

67.   A full study of St Mary's is about to be published: *St Mary's Church, Deerhurst: fieldwork, excavations and structural analysis, 1971-1984*, ed. Philip Rahtz, Lorna Watts, Harold Taylor and Lawrence Butler (Woodbridge, 1997).

68.   Wormald, *How do we know so much about Anglo-Saxon Deerhurst?*, pp. 2-4.

69.   The *Anglo-Saxon Chronicle* says that they met at the island of Alney by Deerhurst; John of Worcester gives Deerhurst as the meeting-place, whence the kings moved to Alney (*JnW* ii, pp. 492-3). See also Williams, 'The Gloucestershire Domesday', p. 16, where the author's inability to proof-read her own material has produced the ludicrous 'Olney (Bucks) near Winchcombe' (*sic*) for the intended 'Alney near Deerhurst'. The site of the meeting was probably the former island later known as the Eight, Naight or Night (presumably from 'eyot', island), just west of Deerhurst and no more than a few minutes walking distance away; the island is now lost through the silting up of the western arm of the river at this point (James D. Harris, 'The site of Alney, AD 1016', *Glevensis: the Gloucester and District Archaeological Research Group Review* no. 26 (1992), pp. 11-12). I owe this reference to Michael Hare.

70.   *GDB*, ff. 163-163v; *DB Gloucs*, nos. 1,24-38, see also Williams, 'A west-country magnate of the eleventh century', cited in note 27 above.

71.   *DB Gloucs*, no. 1,33; in fact the details of the lands assigned to the church amount to 24$^{1}/_{2}$ hides.

72.   The process is rarely recorded, but see, for example, the fate of the Kentish minsters described in Nicholas Brooks, *The early history of the church of Canterbury* (Leicester, 1984), pp. 201-6.

73.   Another west midlands example might be seen in the minster of Wootton Wawen, Warks, founded in the eighth century but held in King Edward's reign by Vagn, a rich thegn in the following of Earl Leofric of Mercia; his name (*Waga* in Domesday Book) is preserved in that of Wootton Wawen ('Vagn's Wootton') itself (Steven Bassett, 'In search of the origins of Anglo-Saxon kingdoms', *The origins of Anglo-Saxon kingdoms*, ed. Steven Bassett (Leicester, 1989), pp. 18-9; *GDB*, fo. 242v; *Domesday Book: Warwickshire*, ed. Judy Plaister (Chichester, 1976), no. 22,9). Vagn attests several documents dating from Edward the Confessor's reign, including S.1425, where he appears as the leader of Earl Leofric's housecarls (see Simon Keynes, 'A lost cartulary of St Albans Abbey', *Anglo-Saxon England* 22 (1993), pp. 266-7).

74.   This is the traditional interpretation of Odda's church, but see now Michael Hare, 'The development of Gloucester as a royal ceremonial centre in the eleventh century', forthcoming, note 165, where it is suggested that the description of the building as a 'royal church' (*regiam aulam*), and its proximity to the minster of St

Mary, might suggest the setting for a royal 'crown-wearing'. I am grateful to Michael Hare for allowing me to read this paper in advance of publication.

75. II Edgar, 1,2; *EHD* i, p. 395, The code distinguishes between demesne-tithes and those paid from the *geneatland*, land whose holders owed service to the lord.

76. John Blair, 'Introduction: from minster to parish church', *Minsters and Parish churches: the local church in transition, 950-1200*, ed. John Blair, Oxford University Committee for Archaeology, Monograph no 17 (Oxford, 1988), pp. 1-19; R. Morris, *Churches in the landscape* (London, 1989), pp. 140-67.

77. Elizabeth Okasha, *Handbook of Anglo-Saxon non-runic inscriptions* (Cambridge, 1971), no. 64. Unlike Odda's church, that of Orm at Kirkdale is recorded in Domesday; it was part of the manor of Kirby Moorside, assessed, with its numerous berewicks, at 56½ carucates, and worth £12 in 1066. Like the rest of Orm's substantial estate (valued at just over £49) it had passed by 1086 to Hugh fitzBaldric (*GDB* fo. 327v; *Domesday Book: Yorkshire*, ed. Margaret Faull and Marie Stinson (Chichester, 1980), no. 23N,19 and note; Clarke, *The English nobility under Edward the Confessor*, pp. 327-8). Kirkdale is another church associated with Archbishop Ealdred of York, since its physical fabric at least might have been influenced by Ealdred's building work at Beverley Minster (R. Morris and E. Cambridge, 'Beverley Minster before the early thirteenth century', *Medieval Art and Architecture in the East Riding of Yorkshire*, ed. C. Wilson, British Archaeological Association Conference Transactions no. 9 (1989), pp. 19-20). I owe this reference to Michael Hare.

78. S.1392-3, 1396-7 (Lyfing), S.1406-9 (Ealdred). S.1406, in which Odda is not entitled *dux*, must date from before his appointment as earl in 1051, and S.1407, which is attested both by Earl Ralph (who appears for the first time in 1050) and by Earl Harold, must date from after Harold's accession to Wessex in 1053, when Odda was compensated with Worcestershire. S.1408-9, which are not attested either by Earl Godwine of Wessex, or by Harold, must date from the period of their exile in 1051-2 (Vanessa J. King, 'Ealdred, archbishop of York: the Worcester years', *Anglo-Norman Studies* 18 (1996), pp. 134-5).

79. S.1391.

80. Robertson, *Anglo-Saxon Charters*, Appendix II, no. 5, pp. 251, 498-9. Michael Lapidge has suggested that the donor might be 'Odda the monk' (presumably of Worcester) who attests S.1058, dated 1044x51 ('Surviving book-lists from Anglo-Saxon England', *Learning and literature in Anglo-Saxon England*, ed. Michael Lapidge and Helmut Gneuss (Cambridge 1985), p. 63; I owe this reference to Michael Hare). S.1058 is a spurious charter of Edward the Confessor granting land at Lench to one Osferth; it comes from the archive of Evesham Abbey and was probably forged at Evesham to provide title to one of its estates at Lench (Atch Lench or Church Lench), both of which were in disputed ownership (*Chronicon Abbatiae de Evesham*, ed. W. Dunn Macray, Rolls Series (London 1863), pp. 72, 84, 86, 94). Some English notes appended to the charter relate to a possibly genuine lease of the same land to Osferth by Lyfing, bishop of Worcester, and it is to this lease that the witness-list belongs. Bishop Lyfing died in March 1046, and since the witnesses include Earl Thuri, the lease

cannot be later than 1045, when Thuri's earldom (the east midlands) passed to Earl Godwine's nephew, Beorn Estrithson (Williams, 'The king's nephew', p. 330). But, as Sir Ivor Atkins pointed out, the two last attestations, 'Odda m' and 'Ælfric m', must be those of Odda of Deerhurst and his brother Ælfric; in these cases 'm' should be extended not as m/onachus/ but as m/inister/ (Sir Ivor Atkins, 'The Church of Worcester from the eighth to the twelfth century', *Antiquaries Journal* 20 (1940), p. 22).

81.   Æthelweard the Chronicler had a copy of Ælfric's *Catholic Homilies*, and both he and his son Æthelmær actively sponsored translations from the Latin, as well as works in English (Campbell, *The Chronicle of Æthelweard*, pp. xiv-xv).

82.   S.1474; Robertson, *Anglo-Saxon Charters*, pp. 200-3; Mary-Anne O'Donovan, *Charters of Sherborne* (Oxford 1988), no. 17, pp. 59-61.

83.   Keynes, *An atlas of attestations in Anglo-Saxon Charters*, Table LXXV.

84.   *GDB*, ff. 101, 101v, 104v, 105, 113v, 114v, 115; *DB Devon*, nos. 1,56; 2,9; 15,3-5:8-10:39-53; 30,1; 35,1:10 and notes. The family was reconstructed by H.P.R. Finberg, 'The house of Ordgar and the foundation of Tavistock Abbey', *English Historical Review* 53 (1943), pp. 190-201; idem, 'Childe's Tomb', *Lucerna* (London, 1964), pp. 186-203.

85.   S.1405; *GDB* ff. 173, 173v; *DB Worcestershire*, nos. 2,24;29,63; see also King, 'Ealdred, archbishop of York', p. 133 and note 83. Dodda also attests a charter of Bishop Lyfing, dated 1042 (S .1396) and his son Beorhtric attests a sale of land in Somerset in 1072 (David A. E. Pelteret, *Catalogue of English post-Conquest Vernacular Documents* (Woodbridge, 1990), no. 56 and see also nos. 11, 144).

NOTES